Mystery in the Stable

Lisa Flinn and Barbara Younger

Illustrated by Judi Niernberger

Abingdon Press

Nashville

Mystery in the Stable

ISBN 0-687-49336-6

06 07 08 09 10 11 12 13 14 15 - 10 9 8 7 6 5 4 3 2 1

Printed in China

Dedicated to Ellie Lind Lewis
and Becky and Nick Younger

"I've counted seven ox carts, one chariot, two Roman soldiers, one camel, and eleven donkeys," Jacob said to his sister, Anna.

Jacob and Anna had climbed to the roof of their house to watch the crowds below. Under the order of Emperor Augustus, all of the people were going to the hometown of their ancestors to be counted.

Travelers were coming to the tiny town of
Bethlehem by every road. Many of these travelers
were descendants of David, the famous king.

As Jacob practiced a new spin with their wooden top, Anna spotted a man leading a donkey through the inn's gate. She thought the young woman on the donkey looked tired. "There's another donkey," Anna called.

"That makes twelve," Jacob called back.

The man knocked on the door of the inn.

Anna saw the innkeeper step out and point to the place where the travelers kept their animals. After the man led the donkey to the stable, he helped the woman to the ground. When the woman lifted a basket from the donkey, Anna could see that it was filled with strips of white linen cloth. The man and the woman went into the stable.

"Jacob, look," Anna said. "That's very puzzling. Why would that woman take a basketful of cloth into the stable where the animals stay?"

"Their donkey might be hurt and need bandaging," Jacob offered.

"Maybe," answered Anna.

Soon the man came back to where the donkey was tied. He took down a bundle of tools from the donkey's back.

"I hear a hammer tapping," said Jacob a few minutes later. "Do you think something is broken?"

"The only thing broken in there is the manger. I saw it yesterday," Anna answered, taking a turn with the top. "But why should that man care? It's only a manger."

"He could be a carpenter," Jacob suggested. "They like to fix things."

Just then the innkeeper's son ran to the
stable clutching a rolled blanket. When
he came out again, he coaxed the donkey
inside.

"I wonder if he knows what's going on,"
said Jacob.

For a time all was quiet. No one came or went. The sun began to set. Anna watched as the innkeeper carried a lamp to the stable. His wife brought a basket of bread and a jug of water.

"That's odd," said Anna. "I've never seen her take supper to the stable before."

"Are they going to sleep in the stable with the animals?" asked Jacob.

"There are so many people in town for the census," Anna replied. "The inn must be full. I guess everybody needs a place to stay."

"Hey," said Jacob, "let's not forget our own supper."

They scrambled down the ladder
and rushed into the house. Jacob and Anna
finished their lentil stew as quickly as they could.

"Can we sleep on the roof tonight?" Anna asked her mother.

"Why tonight?" asked her mother.

"Because there's a mystery in the stable, and we want to solve it," said Anna.

"All right, but stay out of trouble," she told them.

Jacob and Anna climbed back to the rooftop.
The sky was now dark and a breeze blew across the warm clay.

Unrolling their sleeping mats, they chose a spot just right for keeping watch on the stable.

The streets were quiet. Hours passed.

Anna awoke to the sound of men's voices: "We might need to check every stable in the whole city of David!"

She poked her brother.

"Listen," she said as they crawled closer to the edge.

"We're just shepherds, but an angel came to us. So here we are, searching the streets of Bethlehem in the middle of the night."

"The angel told us we would find the Savior in a bed of straw."

Then a boy's voice called out, "I see a light! Over there!"

"Why would they look for the Savior in a stable?" Anna asked. "That doesn't seem right."

"An angel told them to," said Jacob. "I heard a shepherd say that."

"This is getting even more mysterious," Anna said, "and amazing."

As the shepherds reached the stone entrance, Jacob and Anna could finally see them.

"One shepherd has a sheepskin," Jacob reported. "The other has a sack. And the boy is carrying a flute."

"Do you think those are gifts?" Anna asked.

Once the shepherds were in the stable, Jacob and Anna couldn't hear them talking anymore. After awhile, they heard the music of the flute.

When the shepherds left, Jacob and Anna heard them praising God with joyful voices.

"Why are they are so happy?" Anna wondered. "Who did they see?"

"Do you think the man is the Savior?" asked Jacob.

"I wish we could find out for ourselves," said Anna.

"Leave it to me," said Jacob as he grabbed the top, giving it a powerful twist. The top spun to the ledge, wobbled wildly, and fell to the courtyard below.

"I'm going down to get it," said Jacob.

"Not without me, you're not," Anna told him.

Jacob ran over to where the top had come to rest. Anna slipped closer to the stable.

"I can't see much," she whispered to Jacob as he stepped near.

Without a word, Jacob gave the top another powerful twist, sending it spinning through the entry.

"Oh! What's this?" the man called out.

He bent down and scooped up the top.

Jacob and Anna jumped back.

"Aren't you children up late?" asked the man.

"We were sleeping on the roof. We've been watching the excitement down here," Anna explained. "We saw the shepherds come to visit."

"Would you like to see why they came?" asked the man.

Jacob and Anna nodded. The man motioned them in and then turned toward the manger.

The woman was holding a baby. The baby was wrapped in strips of white linen cloth. She laid the baby in the manger and then looked up and smiled at Jacob and Anna.

"A baby!" said Anna.

"We never guessed this was all about a baby," said Jacob. "We didn't see him come in before."

"That's because our son was born this very evening," said the woman.

"An angel told the shepherds to come to Bethlehem to find the Savior. He would be in a bed of straw," said Anna.

"Like your baby," said Jacob.

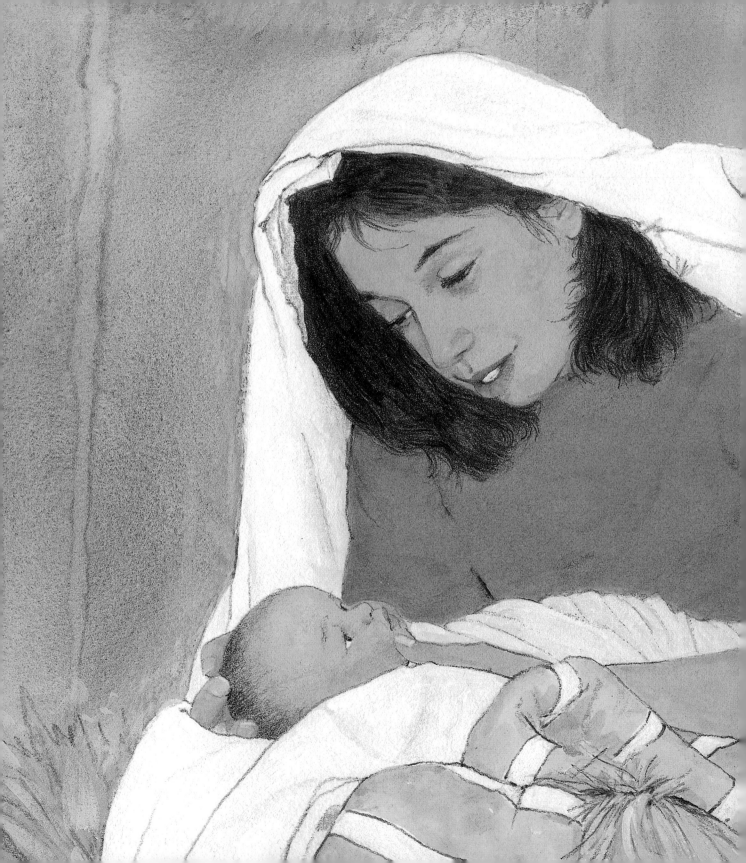

"Does this mean that your baby is the promised Savior?" asked Anna.

"So the angel told us," said the woman. "Isn't he beautiful?"

"He is beautiful," said Jacob, "but he's only a baby! How can he be the Savior?"

"When he grows up," answered the woman, "he will do great things and his kingdom will never end."

Judi Nierenberger

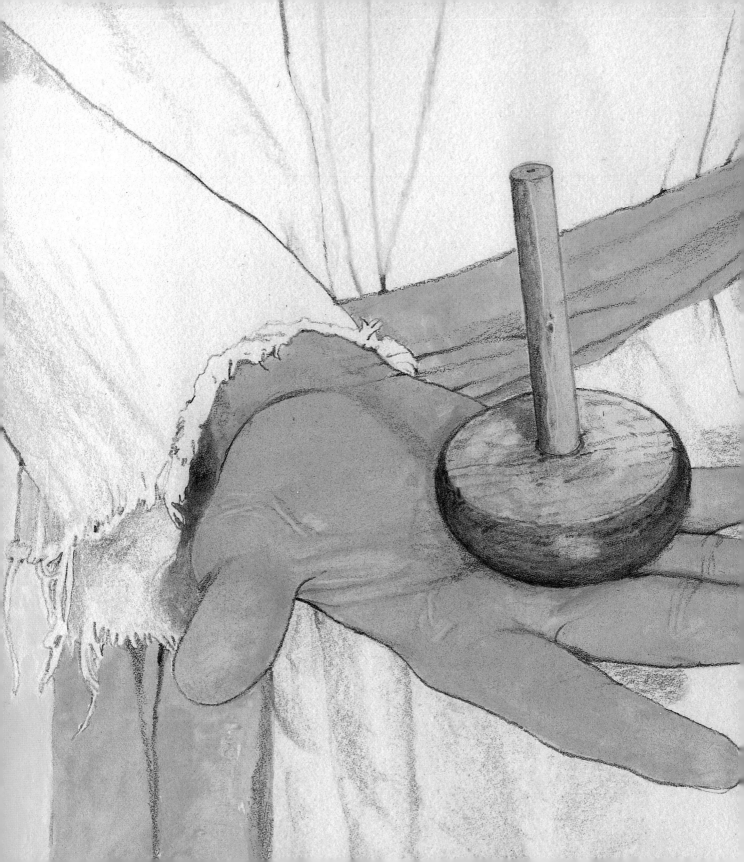

Quietly, Jacob and Anna walked over to where the baby slept. They knelt down to see him better.

Then the man held out the top, "I believe this is yours."

Jacob took the top and turned it slowly in his palm. He glanced at Anna.

"Here," said Jacob, handing the top back to the man. "We want to give this to your baby."

"Thank you," said the man. "Our son will like this."

"We've been watching the stable all day and all night," said Jacob. "We've been trying to figure out what's going on."

"I think I know," said Anna. "The town is crowded. There's no room for you in the inn, so they let you stay in the stable where the travelers keep their animals. The innkeeper brought you a lamp. His wife sent her son with a blanket, and she delivered a basket of food and some water. This is where your baby was born. You wrapped him in those strips of cloth we saw you carry in. Now he's sleeping in the manger you fixed with your hammer."

"The angel sent the shepherds to find the Savior on a bed of straw, somewhere in Bethlehem," added Jacob. "And here he is!"

"Yes, you are quite observant," said the man.

"Indeed you are," said the woman.

"We got to see the Savior!" Jacob said.

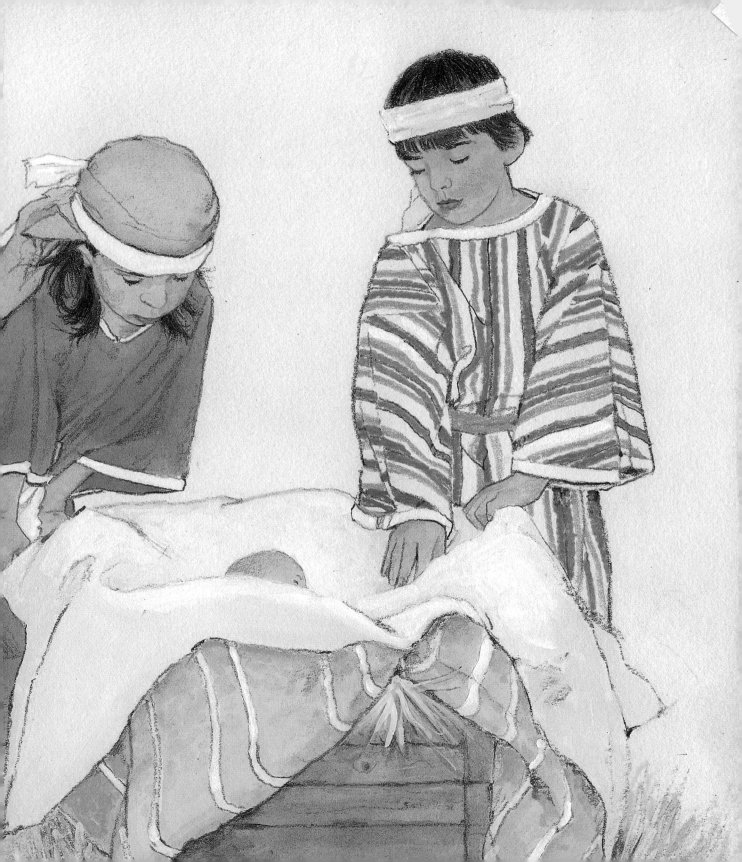

"And," Anna announced, "tonight we solved a mystery, a wonderful mystery, the mystery in the stable."

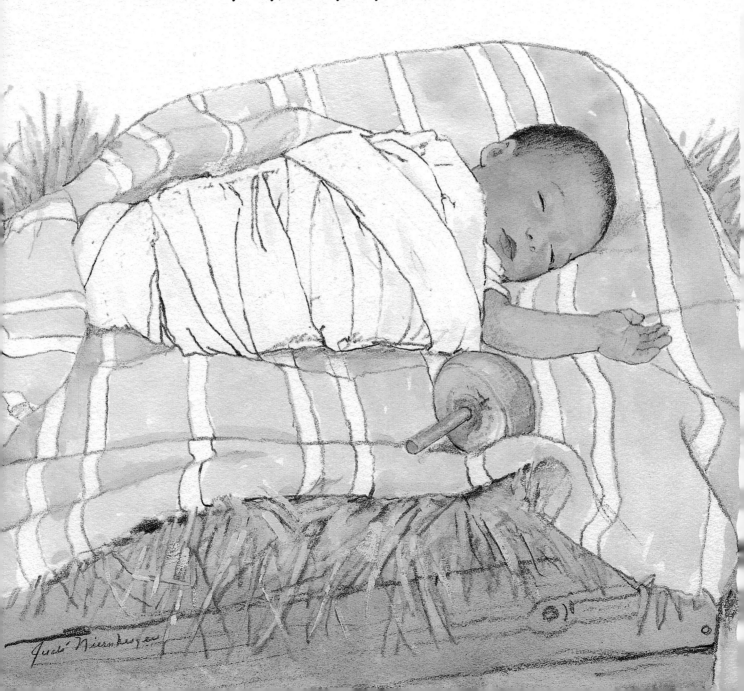